This page intentionally left blank

This page intentionally left blank

This page intentionally left blank

This page intentionally left blank

This page intentionally left blank

This page intentionally left blank

This page intentionally left blank

This page intentionally left blank

This page intentionally left blank

This page intentionally left blank

This page intentionally left blank

This page intentionally left blank

This page intentionally left blank

This page intentionally left blank

This page intentionally left blank

This page intentionally left blank

This page intentionally left blank

This page intentionally left blank

This page intentionally left blank

This page intentionally left blank

This page intentionally left blank

This page intentionally left blank

This page intentionally left blank

This page intentionally left blank

This page intentionally left blank

This page intentionally left blank

This page intentionally left blank

This page intentionally left blank

This page intentionally left blank

This page intentionally left blank

This page intentionally left blank

This page intentionally left blank

This page intentionally left blank

This page intentionally left blank

This page intentionally left blank

This page intentionally left blank

This page intentionally left blank

This page intentionally left blank

This page intentionally left blank

This page intentionally left blank

This page intentionally left blank

This page intentionally left blank

This page intentionally left blank

This page intentionally left blank

This page intentionally left blank

This page intentionally left blank

This page intentionally left blank

This page intentionally left blank

This page intentionally left blank

This page intentionally left blank

This page intentionally left blank

This page intentionally left blank

This page intentionally left blank

This page intentionally left blank

This page intentionally left blank

This page intentionally left blank

This page intentionally left blank

This page intentionally left blank

This page intentionally left blank

This page intentionally left blank

This page intentionally left blank

This page intentionally left blank

This page intentionally left blank

This page intentionally left blank

73

This page intentionally left blank

This page intentionally left blank

This page intentionally left blank

This page intentionally left blank

This page intentionally left blank

This page intentionally left blank

This page intentionally left blank

This page intentionally left blank

This page intentionally left blank

This page intentionally left blank

This page intentionally left blank

This page intentionally left blank

This page intentionally left blank

This page intentionally left blank

This page intentionally left blank

This page intentionally left blank

This page intentionally left blank

This page intentionally left blank

This page intentionally left blank

This page intentionally left blank

This page intentionally left blank